PERA

GATESHEAD PERAMBULATIONS

A collection of stories from centuries ago

Desmond O'Donnell

Drawings by Joyce Webster

Bridge Studios
Northumberland
1990

First published in Great Britain 1990

by Bridge Studios,
Kirklands,
The Old Vicarage,
Scremerston,
Berwick upon Tweed,
Northumberland
TD15 2RB

Tel.: 0289 302658/330274

ISBN 1 872010 20 2

Typeset by EMS Phototypesetting,
Hide Hill, Berwick upon Tweed.

Printed by Martin's of Berwick Ltd.

Contents

Acknowledgements

Acknowledgement is given for information obtained during extensive research amongst the Monthly Chronicles of North Country Lore and Legend, the Friday Books, various histories of Northumberland and Durham, newspaper cuttings and many other sources.

Introduction

The Metropolitan Borough of Gateshead covers a large area. To the north the boundary is the River Tyne and the City of Newcastle, to the south Kibblesworth and Birtley. To the east are Felling, Heworth, Bill Quay and Wardley, to the west Whickham, Swalwell, Blaydon, Winlaton, Ryton, Crawcrook and Rowlands Gill.

Over the years there has been extensive development over the whole area both central and on the outskirts, the latest being the setting up of the 1990 National Garden Festival on a 200 acre site along the riverside, Dunston, Eslington Park and Norwood.

But any extensive development should never blot out past history and in this pocket booklet are collected together just eight of the stories of long ago in the area now covered by this Metropolitan Borough.

Gateshead Perambulations

Perambulations. What a gloriously old-fashioned word, regretfully now practically unused. Even the mothers who push their babies on their daily walk are not truly aware of the derivation of the word 'pram'.

Perambulations; the act of walking about (according to the Oxford Dictionary).

Nearly two hundred years ago there had been an annual Gateshead Perambulations, the walking of the boundaries of the town to establish a right of ownership, but this was discontinued in 1792.

But then came Ascension Day, 27th May, 1824.

The morn was fine, the day was clear,
The sun auspicious shone;
The assembled groups from far and near
Were met at Gateshead Town
To do a thing not often done
Upon Ascension Day.
The thought elated everyone
Dressed up in best array

The perambulators met at St Mary's

Church at nine o'clock in the morning. The church bells rang out and, as always on major occasions on both sides of the Tyne, the guns of the nearby Price's Glassworks were fired. Headed by two pipers and two constables preceding the rector, John Collinson, and his churchwardens, they moved off towards the River Tyne to commence their walk around the boundaries of Gabrosentum, a name by which Gateshead was known in Roman times. Some, the young active ones, determined to proceed around the exact boundaries, climbed down a ladder dropped from the side of the Tyne Bridge and then continued a rather slow laborious path through the slimy mud on the river banks along the town's northern boundary. The rest chose to proceed more sedately along the banks at a higher level. As they walked the western boundaries to Wrekenton the pipers played the Keel Row, surely a Newcastle ditty.

At Wrekenton a stop was made for refreshments, both alcoholic and otherwise, whilst the ladies on the walk entertained everyone with a lively dance. The whole party proceeded onwards along the southern and eastern boundaries of the town until they reached the River Tyne at Friar's Goose. While most of the party continued close to the bank, the pipers, constables and senior citizens climbed into boats to be rowed along the river back to the Tyne Bridge to complete the necessary full circuit of the boundaries of Gateshead. The whole perambulation had taken seven and a half hours.

At half past four the party sat down to dinner at the Black Bull Inn. After dinner a number of copper medals were distributed to commemorate the occasion.

This seems to have been a one-off occasion for the boundaries were not again perambulated until 24th May, 1836, boundary tokens again being struck, these bearing the name of Geo. Hawkes Esq. Mayor, together with the names of five aldermen of Gateshead. In 1849, again on 24th May, George Hawkes was still the mayor, his name again appearing on the token together with those of a further six aldermen and the Town Clerk, William Kell.

One of these tokens turned up in 1876 in a curiosity shop in Edinburgh and because of the discovery of a further token we do know that yet another perambulation did take place in 1857. This particular token is engraved with the words 'Borough of Gateshead Boundary Token' and contains the names of four churchwardens and four overseers.

The story of the token's find is an interesting and amusing one. A Gosforth man called Romler was returning home one day on the tram car when the conductor bitterly complained that a fellow had given him a 'wrang penny', a favourite phrase of conductors in those days who had been given anything but the genuine article. But Mr Romler was no fool and was only too delighted to exchange the token with a new penny much to the relief of the conductor, still complaining about the 'dorty trick' that had been played upon him. Mr Romler, on the other hand, knew what a bargain he had.

But it appears that the perambulation of 5th October, 1857, was the last to take place in Gateshead, all the pity for far too many of these curious customs have disappeared, practically without trace, just like the old buildings, factories and homes of yesteryear. So before the traces completely disappear, let me pen a few more words concerning the places and the people of Old Gateshead and its environs.

The Great Fire at Gateshead

Our next perambulation begins very close to where the last one ended, close to the river and the Tyne Bridge, whilst in time it moves on just twenty years to 6th October, 1854.

Very early on that Thursday morning, in fact just after midnight, a fire began at Hillgate, a street running parallel to the river bank. The worsted factory belonging to Messrs. J. Wilson and Sons contained quite a lot of heavy machinery resting on wooden floors and it took less than one hour for the factory to be completely gutted. But by that time the fire had spread to the next building going east towards the sea, a six-storied building some eighty feet long and twenty feet wide known as Bertram's Warehouse.

Originally it had been used to store the goods of the firm, Bertram and Spencer, but had, for quite some time, been used as a general storehouse for all sorts of goods belonging to various merchants from both Gateshead and Newcastle. Consequently no one could exactly identify its contents but it was said to contain some two hundred tons of iron, eight hundred of lead, one hundred and seventy of manganese, together with various quantities of nitrate of soda, alum, arsenic, copperas, salt, naptha, guano and a massive three thousand tons of brimstone. Gateshead residents were quite aware of the fact that a huge amount of combustible material was stored there, so excitement mounted as onlookers collected to await events.

Fire brigades from both Gateshead and Newcastle were already at the scene of the fire, as was a military detachment of fifty men with their machines from Newcastle Barracks. Streams of vivid blue flames from the sulphur made a spectacular entertainment for hundreds of onlookers on both banks of the Tyne, as well as on the bridges themselves. At that point the fire brigades were very confident that the fire would be contained within the two buildings. It seemed to have been forgotten that much of Hillgate had been burnt down that same month four years earlier, and had been substantially rebuilt.

Besides the spectators, a great number of people were either fighting the fire or trying to save valuable possessions from neighbouring houses threatened by the fire.

Then quite suddenly about a quarter past three, a huge explosion took place. An eye witness described it in these words.

> The air was rent as with voices of many thunders, and filled as with the spume of a volcano. Massive walls crumbled into heaps, blocks of houses tumbled into ruins, windows shattered from their frames far and near, and a shower of burning timber

and crashing stones rained terror, destruction and death on every side.

Alarm spread on both sides of the river as a spectacular fire turned into a major disaster. Keels moored in the Tyne were blown onto the banks, the massive iron High Level Bridge quivered on its pillars, burning piles of brimstone with bricks, stones, wood and metal of every kind were thrown around to fall on onlookers before they could even move away from their viewpoint. Those not killed outright were maimed, bruised, battered and wounded, many seriously. Firemen were crushed where they stood in the narrow roadway that was Hillgate when rubbish fell from the sky by the ton. In many cases death was instantaneous. Others more fortunate rushed naked and shrieking into the street, running they knew not where. A writer was later to pen the words,

> A battlefield could not have yielded a more terrible tragedy. Limbs were torn away, bones fractured, lumps of wood forced into the human body, hot stones buried in the flesh, burning sulphur wrapped around unconscious victims and every conceivable injury inflicted on man, woman and child.

Crushed and scorched bodies of the dead were taken to the police station in Gateshead for identification. The wounded were taken to Newcastle Infirmary and the Gateshead Dispensary.

The immense power of the explosion could be gauged by the fact that it burrowed into solid ground and undermined huge blocks of granite which formed tramways for the carts in Hillgate and it cast these huge stones high above St Mary's Church some three hundred yards away to destroy houses in streets even further afield. These huge blocks, some weighing four or five hundredweight, landed in Oakwellgate, five hundreds yards away, while others cleared the river to destroy houses in Grey Street and Pilgrim Street in Newcastle. Fires began on the Newcastle Quayside and many of the numerous chares (narrow streets) were destroyed. Because the Newcastle fire engines were engaged across the river and the Gateshead ones had been destroyed by explosion and fire, engines were sent from both Shields at the mouth of the river, Sunderland and Durham from the south, Morpeth and Berwick from the north and Hexham from the west.

By dawn the destruction was evident and the flames still unsubdued. By the end of the day the fires on both sides of the river had burnt themselves out, leaving in their wake undescribable destruction. Many of the dead, so badly burnt, were unrecognisable, identified in some cases only by their signet rings, keys, a cigar case and, in the case of one of the firemen, by the nozzle of the engine pipe embedded in his bones. It had been an horrific forty-eight hours.

The inquest was adjourned several times and eventually closed on 2nd November. The cause of the explosion remained a mystery although it was generally agreed that no explosives had been illegally stored in the warehouse. Various causes were claimed, sulphur and nitre exploded in reaction to the water poured on them, a mixture of gases from the various chemicals caused them to explode. The inquest jury returned a verdict that 'the death of Thomas Scott and others occasioned by the accidental explosion of a quantity of nitrate of soda and sulphur ... The immediate cause of the explosion was a fire in the worsted mill ... but in what way the two substances which caused the explosion, acted or re-acted, chemically or mechanically, we are unable to decide.'

And it was left only to rebuild Hillgate for the second time in less than five years, while caring for the permanently injured and mourning for the dead.

The Last Cutty Factory

Not far from the scene of the Great Fire of Gateshead is High Street with its supermarkets, office blocks, departmental stores and car parks, a far cry from days long ago, when one of the strangest factories in a narrow street off High Street was nearing its end.

Nowadays one passes over the Tyne Bridge from Newcastle on the way south and before you know it you are on a roadway on stilts over the top of it and it is gone forever. Time was when in order to do the same journey you had to travel up the High Street, and hard lines if you were in a hurry. As your car crawled up the steep street inch by inch in a near traffic jam you had ample time to look around you. Even so, I doubt if you would have noticed King William Street going off the High Street.

Even if, some seventy years ago, you had walked up High Street you would probably not have noticed it then, which, indeed, would have been a great pity. For if you had strolled through the narrow archway at the top of a flight of stairs you would have actually been in King William Street. So what was so remarkable about King William Street those many years ago. Well in that street the very last cutty

KING WILLIAM STREET
GATESHEAD.

factory in the country was about to close down. And what, I know you are dying to ask, is a cutty factory? It is said that silly questions get silly answers. A cutty factory is a place where cutties are made. And if you are now going to ask what a cutty is, then you are not a senior citizen of Geordieland.

Long before the days when cigarettes and briar pipes were popular, one had a smoke from a cutty ... yes, now you have it, a clay pipe. However, if you lived high up the social scale you smoked a churchwarden. In between the cutty and the churchwarden were many other varieties of clay pipes.

If you had spoken to the factory owner, Mr Stonehouse, he would have told you how, in the 1880s he was an apprentice in a Midlands factory where over two hundred men were employed making clay pipes. The demand was so great that this factory was only one of many throughout the country. So it was that Mr Stonehouse moved from the Midlands and set up his own factory in King William Street in Gateshead. And let us go back in time and take a look into his dark, damp and unaired factory, five or six rooms in a street mainly consisting of homes in a narrow alleyway with the rather grand name, which was, I regret to say, the only grand thing about the street.

Push open the door and gingerly walk into the room for its dim light is little help to safe progress. Disappearing into the darkness in front of you is a flight of stairs. Go through the door to your right and you will see pile upon pile of bricks of clay, pipe-clay, hard as stone and just arrived from far off Cornwall. The bricks must first be moistened, 'pug milled' and 'tempered' before they can be made into the exact shape of the pipe. In racks around the room you will see thousands of these clays ready to be baked in the big kiln in the room next door. In this kiln the bricks are fired for twelve hours to make them capable of withstanding the heat of burning tobacco.

Across the passageway in the room on the left is the pug mill where the moistened clay is churned by machine until it is in the exact state to be made into the pipes themselves. This was a far cry from the days before the advent of the machine, when the clay was placed on a bench and pounded with an iron bar in a long hard operation. Out into the passageway again and gingerly mount the stairs for the treads are now none too safe, as it will not be long now before it is finally vacated and demolished.

Push open the door on the left and you will find yourself in a small workshop that looks as if it has been there for centuries. Here Mr Stonehouse, his wife and an assistant sit at their benches. In front of them are partly formed clays looking rather like a bunch of bananas. They have already been rolled into this shape by a rather fascinating process. Try placing a piece of clay in each hand and roll them quickly into the shape of two bananas at the same time, not as easy to do as it at first appears in writing.

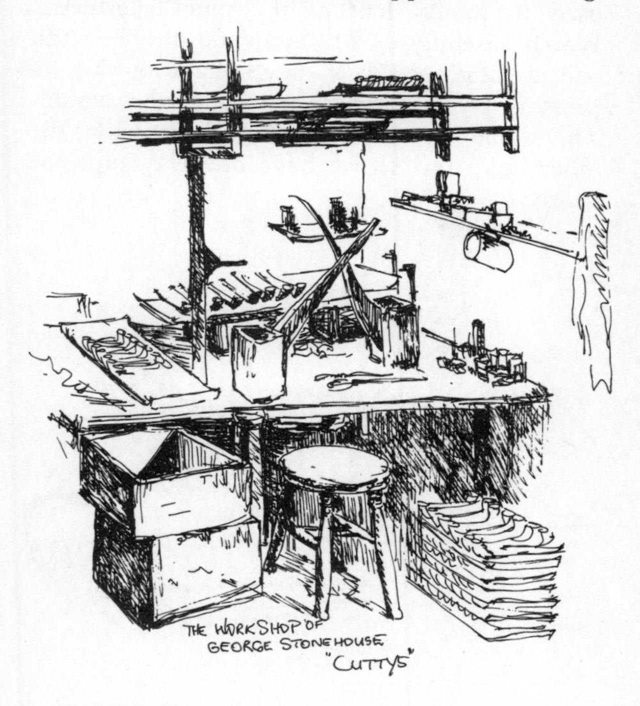

These rough shapes are to go into the moulds, of which some thirty or forty stand ready on the shelves. All are different shapes and sizes, some even now out of fashion and never used. All have names. There are Niggar Heads, Rustics, Ladies Heads, Dukes, Countesses, Buffalo Heads and many more besides, each with their own unique shape. Each is made of steel in two parts, each part being used to mould half of the pipe lengthwise. Watch carefully as Mr Stonehouse places into one of these moulds a rough shape of clay. A press is brought down on top of the mould. The same procedure takes place with the other half, and so we have one clay pipe, or nearly so.

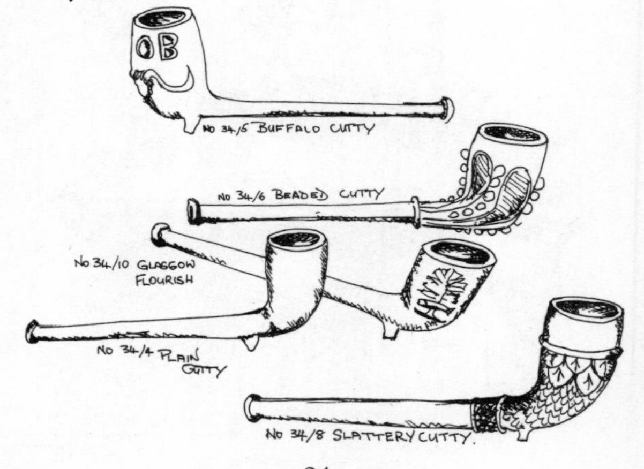

All that is now required is the hole in the middle. Now how do you put a hole in the middle of a clay pipe, especially one like the Churchwarden which was about twenty-four inches long, with no machinery to help with accuracy?

Again watch Mr Stonehouse carefully. He has a long steel rod in his right hand which he pushes through the middle, or appears to do so. But this he tells us would just be disaster. In fact he holds the rod quite still and pulls the pipe stem, damp and wiggly, onto the rod, rather like a lady pulling a silk stocking onto her leg. And when the clay is dried and the mould is removed, all that remains is to trim off the rough edges left by the mould and tip the pipe, that is putting the little red colouring on the end of the stem. Some are even tipped in black for use at funerals. And that is it.

If you are careful not to drop it, the cutty will give you years of use, and the smoking of tobacco will be far better with a cutty than with a new-fangled briar.

But the factory has long since been pulled down, and King William Street as well. As the years have passed shops have risen on the cutty factory's site, have in turn been pulled down, and other establishments have occupied newer premises. And the cutties? The clay pipes? They are no longer popular with most pipe smokers but you can still buy them if you know where the right shop is in Gateshead.

B.R. Stands For...

Before the building of the Gateshead and Felling By-Pass from the Tyne Bridge to the Sunderland area, Gateshead High Street, mentioned in The Last Cutty Factory story, joined on to Sunderland Road. Although the first part of Sunderland Road has now disappeared under fly-overs, concrete pillars and roundabouts, the following stretch remains, still a thriving district of houses, shops and churches.

Let us then continue our perambulations and pass along it until we reach the yellow M, which tells us we have reached Felling Metro Station (or should it be platform).

Have you ever been onto Felling Station lately? I deliberately say 'onto' and not 'into' for a rather special reason. Felling Station is one of the Metro stops on the Newcastle to South Shields part of the system, with its orange and cream livery and complete lack of character. One approaches the platform from the road by a narrow pedestrian bridge, and then down a steep slope to come face to face with the modern technology of graffiti covered ticket machines. Once on the inadequate canopied platform one realises the bareness of it all, the coldness, the ... nothingness. Even the pre-Metro diesel trains ignore it, passing through the back door, so as to speak, without even an acknowledgement of the station's existence as they speed onwards to Sunderland.

But it was not always so. I well remember in the early 1930s, as a young boy going into Felling Station ... yes, into not onto ... on my monthly visit to my Auntie Clare in Elliott Street, a part of Sunderland Road parallel to the railway line, which is now a rather attractive grass slope, ablaze with flowers in the summer. In those days Felling Station was part of the L.N.E.R. system, the London and North Eastern Railway for the benefit of the younger generation.

My brother, Leo, my sister, Eileen and I looked forward with great anticipation at the end of our visit to going into the station. I well remember being thrilled to run over the line and down the slope to the platform by means of a covered glass sided tunnel, which echoed to our deliberately noisy footsteps. Our goal was to be the first onto the platform itself. This housed a mass of interesting places, the waiting rooms with their blazing log and coal fires, the station master's and ticket collector's offices, the left luggage office, the booking office, with its strangely latticed window, the toilets and much more besides.

Even after those, there was much more to capture our attention. There were the chocolate machines to use, with pennies begged from our parents. There were those fascinating coloured posters imploring us to visit the far away seaside resorts of Skegness and Scarborough, accessible through the railway system. Vying with them for attention were those attractive tin advertisements, persuading us to buy tea, coffee, cocoa, chocolate and a vast array of food and drink. Everywhere in Felling Station there was character, liveliness, vitality, a veritable wonderland for old and young alike.

And now it is all gone. Even the stone entrance on Elliott Street was demolished, including the engraving above it. It included, if my memory serves me correctly, the letters B.R., not surprisingly you may think because it stands for British Rail. Ah, but British Rail had never been heard of in the days when the stone was first erected, as the railway network throughout the country was still known by the initial letters of the various companies making up the total rail network of the country.

So what then did B.R. stand for? Across the tracks slightly to one side of the Metro platform stands a small building, until comparatively recent years rather dilapidated. Its windows have been replaced, its stonework cleaned a little and it was used for several years as a small museum, before being put up for sale. You might just make out the letters B.R. engraved on the stonework, together with a coat of arms and what looks like a candle in an old fashioned candlestick. For all the world it looks like a lodge of a gentleman's house, but it is not, and never has been.

This building is one of the oldest and most interesting disused railway stations in the country and few people give it even a first glance, let alone a second. I wonder how many of the residents of the modern blocks of flats or the drinkers at the nearby Mulberry Inn nearly opposite the old railway station know of the connection between those two buildings.

B.R. stands for Brandling Railway and the building is the old Brandling Station, the candle above the letters and the coat of arms being the burning brand of that famous Northumbrian family. In 1721 the Brandlings, the Bowes of Gibside, the Russells of Brancepeth and others were all powerful coal owners, who were able because of the higher price paid for their coal in London to dictate the price of coal to the smaller land owners. It was most important to transport their coal quickly and efficiently down to the River Tyne for shipping to London.

This body of coal owners laid down wagon-ways in all directions from all their pits down to the various coal staiths on the River Tyne, including the one renovated for the Gateshead Garden Festival in 1990. In 1845, Robert William Brandling and his brother, John, obtained an Act of Parliament to make a railway from Gateshead to South Shields and Monk-wearmouth to be known as the Brandling

Junction Railway. A start was made at Felling in the August of 1836 and before long the first cargo of coals was carried along the line from the Andrews House Colliery to South Shields for shipping onward to London. An extension to this railway was later constructed to go to Redheugh, Oakwellgate, Hillgate and onward down to the River Tyne staiths.

At this point it was decided that a railway station had to be built at Felling and this was duly opened in 1842. The Brandling Junction Railway became one of the most important in the country, eventually being bought by the Newcastle and Darlington Railway Company, which in 1854 became the North Eastern Railway Company. With the increased traffic a larger station had to be built close to the original one, but it was not very long before it also was too small. It was demolished and an even larger station was built on the same site. That station was the Felling Station I visited each month.

Now most of that station has disappeared and only the platform foundations remain, on which the present day impersonal embellishments have been erected. The steam trains have gone too, the diesels ignore it and no doubt the future electrics will look at it with disdain.

But across the tracks still stands the Brandling Railway Station, close on 150 years old and outliving all the others. Still it proudly shows off its burning brand and its initials, B.R., for all to see who wish to look. There are, I would think, very few of those at the moment. Maybe, in the future, there may be a few more now the history has been re-told.

The Brandlings of Felling Hall

Our next perambulation takes us only the matter of a few yards from the old Brandling Station across the road to the Mulberry Public House and the adjacent housing estate. Centuries ago this area was the beautiful grounds of a beautiful house stretching south towards the River Tyne. So what is the connection between Brandling Station and the Mulberry? The answer to the question is a third building which is no longer there, Felling Hall.

Felling Hall stood between the present railway lines and the River Tyne. Practically all the land in this area belonged, in the middle of the sixteenth century, to the hall's owner, Sir Robert Brandling. He was the forefather of the Brandlings of later years, who owned the railway which transported their coal from their mines down to the staiths on the River Tyne for shipment to London. Felling Hall continued to be the home of the Brandling family for a further two hundred years.

In the year 1760 Charles Brandling felt that the hall, to say the least, was a little past its best for such an important family. In any case he had taken a fancy to live in the fashionable district of Gosforth across the river in Newcastle, a district that had not yet been ravished by the demands of industry. So he had himself built a lovely mansion in what we know now as Gosforth Park.

After the Brandling family had moved into their new stately home, Felling Hall rapidly deteriorated. Bit by bit the walls began to crumble. The once lovely gardens became weed-ridden and full of everyone's rubbish. The weather and the vandals...yes, they were there in those days as well...took their toll until only one part of the hall was of any use at all. It was converted for a far different use and called the Mulberry Inn, so named because one of the Stuart kings on a visit to Felling Hall planted a mulberry tree in the grounds.

This original Mulberry Inn was demolished in the early 1900s and the present Mulberry Inn was later built on a site quite close to the original.

Parts of the old Felling Hall were used to build some of the houses that were built around the Mulberry Inn. A door here, a window there, a few stones here and there were used, not that anyone ever noticed or, I suspect, even cared that a little bit of history was being built into their houses. Even in 1930 one part of Felling Hall still remained. Well, not actually the hall itself, but the summer house which Charles Brandling had built shortly before he moved away from the estate to Gosforth. It stood to the north of the hall in the middle of some beautiful woods. It even remained there when the trees were torn from the ground to make way for the 'modern' housing estate. It still stood when the new school was built, even though the grass around the summer house was concreted over for use as a children's playground. The locals nicknamed it 'Brandling Tower'.

But even it could not go on forever and nothing now remains to remind us of one of the great stately homes of the area. A little green does still remain where the hall stood close to those 'modern' houses of Easten Gardens, now not so modern. The new school, referred to as the Low Board School, was pulled down some fifteen years ago to be replaced by the modern Brandling County Primary School, retaining the famous name at least. The new Mulberry Inn still stands. The tree is not to be seen anywhere. The inn serves the residents of the housing around it as did the old one.

But what is left to remind us of Felling Hall and the Brandling family, who were greatly respected in their time by the people of Felling. Not a lot, I am sorry to say. There is the Brandling Railway Station and the family crest nearly worn off by the weather, but when I showed it to people in the area no one could really tell about its significance to Felling, although the front of the building does now display a plaque explaining its original use.

The officials of Felling Urban District Council had ensured the Brandling name would go on, when they were far sighted enough to adopt the burning brand of the family as their official crest. They were not to know that about two hundred years after the family moved out of Felling, they themselves would be swallowed up by a bigger authority in the name of progress. There are a few streets, Brandling Court, Brandling Place and Brandling Lane, while, practically on the site of the Felling Hall Estate is the Brandling Hall Community Centre. And that as far as I can ascertain is just about that, although there is a Summer Street. I wonder if it really has anything to do with the summer house.

Strange then, that around the Gosforth area

we have Brandling House in Gosforth Park, two Brandling Arms and a Brandling Villa, all three being thriving public houses. And there is Brandling Village itself, a small area practically lost in its larger Gosforth neighbourhood. There should be a moral somewhere, I suspect.

A Factory Before Its Time

Whereas our last perambulation around the estate of the Brandling family was only a short distance from the previous one at the Brandling Railway Station, to reach our next point we need to go westward past the Garden Festival Site and Gateshead's pride and joy, the Metro Centre Shopping Complex, close to which is the area of Swalwell and Whickham. Here on Market Lane is a public house called the Crowley Hotel, whilst close by is Crowley Road with Crowley Avenue a little further away. A mile or so onward near to Winlaton is Crowley Gardens, all connected by name to a factory before its time.

Crowley's Crew may sound like something taking part in the Head of the River Races on an August Bank Holiday Monday, or even in the River Tyne Races, part of the National Garden

Festival in Gateshead. Crowley's Crew were employees of a factory that was two hundred and fifty years before its time. Let me explain.

Long ago one of the most important industries south of the River Tyne was iron and steel, and the most important works belonged to Messrs. Crowley, Millington and Company at both Winlaton and Swalwell. The founder of the firm, Ambrose Crowley, first began work as an anvil maker in the Midlands town of Dudley in the county of Staffordshire. There he made enough money to encourage him to set up his own factory, so he travelled north to Sunderland, where he set up a factory making iron goods, mainly household utensils. But his factory on the banks of the River Wear was never the success he imagined it would have been, so about the year 1690 he closed it down.

He travelled north to Winlaton and there he set up another factory. His advert in a local paper stated that:

> at his works in Winlaton any good workman who can make the following goods shall have constant employment and their wages every week punctually paid, namely, augers, bed-screws, box and sad irons, chains, edge tools, files, hammers, hinges, locks, nails, patten rings and almost every other sort of Smith's Ware.

The confidence in himself was to be fully justified for when Sir Ambrose Crowley died in London in 1713 he left £200,000, a number of valuable estates and a factory which, I am certain, was well ahead of its time.

What made this works so remarkable at the time was, not the products made there, but the way in which Ambrose Crowley organised his work force and the good it did for the inhabitants of Winlaton. In the course of time he turned a few deserted cottages into a thriving town. He turned a factory into a community. He placed the workforce of his factory way ahead of any other workmen in comfort, in education and in intelligence. Everyone at the works, be they workmen or management, was governed by a strict set of rules, which bound all the employees together with common family ties. Every man employed at the factory from the humblest employee to the boss himself was registered.

Not only was a record kept of his name and address, but his age, height, weight, complexion, place of birth, details of parents and numerous unusual statistics like hobbies, interests and even whether or not he smoked a pipe, cigarettes or not at all, were all recorded. Details were also kept of the unusual events that took place during the life of the firm's employees. So it was that we learned that a certain employee, Anne Partridge of Dudley, got into debt and ran away from home and work. Today, no doubt trades unions would be up in arms, complaining of the intrusion into the private lives of employees, and the Council of Civil Liberties would have had Ambrose up in court.

All correspondence to and from the firm was dealt with by a Committee of Survey, who had a most unusual way of dating its correspondence. They did not use the normal year calendar, but instead everything was based on the number of weeks the firm had been in existence, number one being the week the factory opened. So the last letters sent out by this amazing firm were 'dated' week 9,234, giving the factory a life of over 177 years which, in fact, is about five years less than the closing and opening dates given in other records.

Next to this Committee of Survey was a second unusual one. It was the firm's council, made up of all members of the Survey Committee, plus the cashier, the warekeeper and the iron keeper. This committee was an exceptionally powerful one, as it dealt with both criminal and civil matters. Any employee guilty of bad workmanship was brought before it. So were disputes both inside and outside the factory, if they concerned employees of the firm. It settled any arguments about debts of employees and was even empowered to recover debts of one employee to another.

It disciplined an employee breaking factory laws, especially in matters of safety. In the event of anything having to be settled by public courts, it secured legal rights cheaply for employees, and in some extreme cases paid all fees outright. With very rare exceptions, orders made by the council and penalties issued by them were very effective. So it was that the Council became better known by the nickname of 'Crowley's Court'.

Perhaps modern workmen might dispute the right of such a court to have such massive powers, but the employees themselves, from the lowest to the highest, had the greatest of trust in the strict fairness of this court. But not only did the company deal with all legal matters, but also with social problems. Ample provision was made for those who were sick. An amount of ninepence in the pound, just under 4% on average, was taken from all employees' wages and the revenue used to feed, house and clothe the old and permanently disabled, and to provide an allowance each week for all those unable to work through illness. And all this two and a half centuries before anyone ever thought of the National Health Service, Superannuation or the Old Age Pension.

Incidentally, the pensioners were known as Crowley's Poor and wore a badge on their left arm which had the words moulded on it, not one of Crowley's better ideas, I would suggest.

Then there was Crowley's School, where the

children of all employees were superbly educated. The schoolteacher was paid out of the wages of the employees, who weekly paid 2½*d*, which amount also paid for the chaplain, for the schoolroom was used as a church on Sundays. The first chaplain of the factory was listed as Revd Edward Lodge, who later became the headmaster of the Royal Grammar School in Newcastle. The nearby Ryton Church set aside the gallery for the exclusive use of the workmen of the factory, an arrangement made with the church authorities by the factory council.

In 1819 the factory opened a library in Winlaton for the exclusive use of employees and their families, starting with a huge collection of 3,000 books. Sir Ambrose Crowley is said to have introduced freemasonry to the north of England, which is rather doubtful. Nevertheless he did form the first factory branch in the country.

Such then was Crowley's Factory, surely the forerunner of any worker participation industry in the country. It was truly a factory before its time, well before its time. Ambrose Crowley introduced so much that was new to industry, so much that was appreciated by all his employees, and so much that was socially good. His employees were top of the world, the envy of every other workman for miles around. But then things began to go wrong.

Crowley's Crew, as the employees became known throughout the area, became a law unto themselves, the terror of Tyneside, perhaps another first, the first 'bovver boys'. If they thought something was wrong they considered themselves above the law and perfectly entitled to put matters right without recourse to the law. For example, on one occasion they considered that food being sold in Newcastle was far too dear. So they marched in a body into town, took over the market carts, sold all the goods to the public at what they considered reasonable prices, and then, when all the goods had been sold, handed the money they had collected and the carts back again to their owners. The local constabulary stood by and did nothing.

Many other examples of the attitudes of Crowley's Crew were often quoted. It goes probably without saying that they were very politically minded, belonging to the Newcastle Radicals and could often be seen sporting their green and white favours, like modern soccer supporters. After one rally on 11th October, 1819, the Mayor of Newcastle wrote to the Home Secretary saying;

It is impossible to contemplate the meeting

of the 11th inst. without awe, more especially if my information is correct. Seven thousand of them were prepared with arms concealed to resist the civil powers. These men came from a village three miles from town, and there is strong reason to believe that the arms they used were manufactured there.

He was not wrong, for the men did make an assortment of weapons there and were quite prepared, if necessary, to use their home-made articles to assist the election of the popular candidate at voting time. Maybe, in this unsavoury side of the factory, they were also well ahead of their time.

After reaching great heights, Crowley's firm went rapidly downhill, eventually closing in 1872. But was it a factory before its time? I wonder, with its Crowley's Court, Crowley's School, Crowley's Church, Crowley's Poor, Crowley's Superannuation Fund, Crowley's Unemployment Benefit, Crowley's Old Age Pension, Crowley's Library and Crowley's Crew, perhaps it was. Indeed no, it most certainly was.

But today, well over one hundred years after the factory of Sir Ambrose Crowley closed and over two hundred and fifty years after his death, who, in the area of Blaydon, Winlaton or

Swalwell knows about Crowley's Crew or even about the name itself. The frequenters of a certain hostelry and the residents of certain streets will certainly know the name well, of course, but what about the stories behind the name, I wonder. Crowley, who did so much, has it seems been forgotten. Maybe, now, the fault has been rectified. I would like to think so.

Saltwell Park

Perambulations, especially the long ones, tire, and tired people require rest. Where better to obtain it than a couple of miles east at Saltwell Park, the most beautiful of all the North East's public parks, at least in my opinion.

The vast area of which the park is just a part was originally known as Saltwellside and was owned by the Ravensworth family, whose wealth was built mainly on the coal mining industry. A succession of owners followed, led by Robert Brigham and the Hedworths of Harraton, who had a large mansion as their residence towards the end of the Elizabethan era. The Hedworths sold it to William Hall, whose son, Sir Alexander Hedworth, passed it on to his brother. And so the selling and buying went on until eventually the land began to be parcelled off in lots.

Each purchaser had his own mansion on these villa sites, the four main ones being Saltwell Hall, Saltwell Towers, Saltwell Cottage and Ferne-Dene House. Even so the various sites continued to have a variety of owners. Saltwell Park was owned in the mid-nineteenth century by a William Henry Lambton, who, in 1853, sold the estate to William Wailes, who was to be the very last private owner of the land. He was a prominent artist in stained glass and it was he who built the house on the land. The whole of the northern part of the estate was entirely fields, while the southern portion below and around the house was laid out as gardens.

As Mr Wailes became older it was necessary to sell the estate, which was bought in 1876 by the Gateshead Corporation for £32,000. Mr Wailes, however, retained the right to live in the house until he died, his death taking place in 1881 at the age of 72 years. After his death the house was occupied by Mr J. A. D. Shipley, who is remembered in Gateshead because of the magnificent Shipley Art Gallery in the town.

The Gateshead Corporation began to develop the fifty-two acre site shortly after its purchase by making the north part of the estate into attractive grounds rather than the original fields. The first of three bowling greens was laid out in 1878, the other two following in 1887 and 1900. In 1880 a four and a half acre lake was developed, in the centre of which was built an island, onto which a bandstand was placed in 1907. An aviary was built close to the flower garden and maze, which Wailes had himself built before his death. The initial re-development of the estate having being completed, the park was opened in the June of 1876. Development of the park has continued ever since, and yet in much of it one can easily see those first steps.

So what of this park today in which we are to rest from our perambulations of Gateshead. Saltwell Park is a quiet oasis amongst the busy streets which surround it on all sides, noisy with the constant hum of traffic. The southern part is still the garden of the estate, attractively and beautifully laid out with lawns and flower beds close to the Dene with its small but pleasant waterfall splashing playfully down towards its southern boundary.

At this extreme is the Salte Welle, built in 1872, which regretfully today is not as well looked after as the rest of the park, being covered in graffiti and much the worse for wear. Its inscription,

1872
Salte Welle
"DRINKING WELL"
SALTWELL PARK

read with great difficulty, says:–

Whosoevre drynketh of thys water
shall thirste agayne
But whosoevre drynketh of the water that
CHRIST
shall give him
shall nevr be more a thirste
but the water HE shall geve him
shall be the welle of water
sprinyng unto everlasting lyfe

Regretfully the water has not flowed for many a long year unlike when it was first erected in 1872.

Towards the north, not far from the Salte Welle is another fountain, the Charlton Memorial Drinking Fountain engraved with the words;

To George Charlton Esq., J.P., Mayor of Gateshead 1874 and 1875 in recognition of labours in the cause of Social Reform.

This memorial has four drinking troughs, but, like the Salte Welle, as dry as bone and have been for some time. There are other statues and memorials in the park. Near the main entrance is a small one inscribed to Alderman John Lucas.

Born Dec. 7, 1837. Died Aug 2, 1900. Erected by public subscription 1903.

In the centre of the park is the South African War Memorial with the Angel of Peace, unveiled on 11th November, 1905, on top. It bears an attractive poem attributed to Collins and written in 1746.

How sleep the brave who sink to rest
By all their country's wishes blest.
By fairy hands their knell is rung.
By form unseen their dirge is sung.

The newest memorial is in the form of a peaceful seating area and was dedicated on 12th July 1981,

In memory of 1,419 officers and other ranks who laid down their lives in the wars between 1900 and 1945, each a son of the 9th Battalion the Durham Light Infantry T.A.

It is made from stones recovered from the Drill Hall in Burt Terrace in Gateshead when it was demolished.

The centrepiece of the park is the original mansion, Saltwell Towers, a once impressive building, which over the years has fallen into decay. Now, thankfully, it is being restored and although at the time of writing is but a shell, I trust that in due course it will return to something near to its former glory.

So the whole of this southern area is one of history, plus modern beauty in the form of lovely lawns, flower beds, shrubs and trees. On the other hand the northern part in the main is much as it was in days gone by, a wide grassy space with the lake more or less as it was. Hired rowing boats now move amongst the swans, but perhaps they did so in 1880 as well. Close to the lake, however, there are concessions to modern times in the form of a children's play area with mini Honda bikes, a kiddies castle, roundabouts, swings and slides. A brightly coloured old aeroplane towers above this area, a Viking 700, I am told, which was in service from 1952 to 1972 and in which Winston Churchill, the country's war time Prime Minister, flew. Today children are permitted to sit in the cockpit, go down the escape chute and sit in the passenger seats of this old aircraft, now in the livery of the Saltwell Airways. Close by is the North Lodge, built in 1882, and still used as a residence, and, in the same style, another house now used as the base for the Parks Department staff. Next door is the small animals house and not too far away a well designed infants' play area, with a home for goats and chickens, amidst well appointed flower beds ablaze with colour in the summer.

This then is the Salte Welle Park of over a century ago and the Saltwell Park of the present day, a place to take a break from our Gateshead Perambulations.

But now we must perambulate our greatest distance right across the Metropolitan Borough of Gateshead to Blaydon to discover the story behind the best known tune in the North East of the country.

The Blaydon Races

If one goes westward along the banks of the River Tyne through Blaydon, one soon comes to the huge Stella Power Station in front of which is a green grassed field, one of the many sites of the Blaydon Races. And the others? Well, perhaps, we should start the Blaydon Races story at the end, which is not quite as ridiculous as it at first sounds.

> There were lots of lads and lasses there
> all with smiling faces,
> Gannin alang the Scotswood Road
> te see the Blaydon Races.

Those are the famous lines of a famous song, a song which made a local event into an international institution, which, but for the song, would have passed unnoticed into oblivion. But despite the great fame of the song, how many who hear it really know very much about the actual Blaydon Races?

The year was 1916, the middle of the First World War, which had caused the cancellation of all horse racing meetings throughout the country. The full production of the Armstrong Whitworth's factory on Scotswood Road had been turned over to the machines of war. But because the factory had been so successful and the workers had strived hard for nearly two years, they were allowed to have two days' holiday, during which they were permitted to have a two-day race meeting at Blaydon on Friday and Saturday, 1st and 2nd September. The Friday meeting had been a huge success and on the Saturday morning the sun was still shining as it had been on the previous day. So thousands made their way to Blaydon Races, the thought of a second day's excellent sport being uppermost in their minds. As the racegoers watched the first race of the day, none of them could possibly have realised that they were watching the end of the Blaydon Races.

But the date quoted in the song, 9th June,

1862, was not anyway near the start of the Blaydon Races. They were started by the keelmen of Newcastle who, every Christmas, went sword dancing to raise money to be used as a prize for the Keelmen's Purse, a race for both horses and donkeys, which was held every year during the Hoppings (the local fayre) on the Guards at Blaydon. As the years went by the keelmen became fewer in number as the work on the keels (boats) on the River Tyne became less needed.

Consequently they found increasing difficulty in raising enough money. Perhaps the races would have ended because of that, but it was the coming of the railway to Blaydon which eventually caused it, because it was built on that flat piece of land that was the racecourse.

So from 1836, when the station was built, the races were forgotten for twenty-six years until a small group of people decided to revive the event. They realised that they could draw quite good crowds if they sited the racecourse somewhere within easy reach of Blaydon Station and, if possible, with easy road and river transport. They found the ideal site right in the middle of the River Tyne. Blaydon Island stands in the river close on the north side to the small hamlet of Bell's Close and on the south side to the factories near to the Scotswood Bridges. Today the site is mainly occupied by the works of the Anglo Great Lakes Corporation covering close on one hundred acres. In the mid nineteenth century it was an ideal grassy place.

So on Whit Monday, 20th May, 1861, the Blaydon Races re-started. The racegoers travelling by rail to Blaydon Station came across a row of barges to the island, whilst the horses waded across the Tyne at Bell's Close. Special trains were laid on and a race omnibus ran from Newcastle. Several steamers made the journey from the river mouth at Shields.

The re-opening day was a huge success and the local press afterwards carried numerous accounts of the event. Tucked away at the bottom of the page was another item, given very little prominence. It told of a concert at the Mechanics' Hall at Blaydon featuring comic and sentimental songs by a certain Mr Ridley. No one at the time was to know that it was the same Mr Ridley, who would later go down in history for the fact that everyone knows about the Blaydon Races, locally, nationally, and internationally. Geordie Ridley had attended the re-opening meeting and shortly before the following year's meeting wrote the song, which he sang a week before that meeting, which took place on 9th June 1862.

He sang it at the Wheatsheaf Music Saloon,

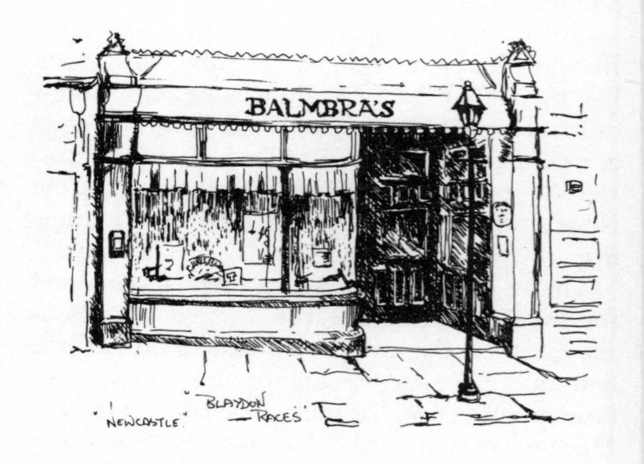

better known after its landlord as Balmbras. It was from there that the buses ran to the races. The bus in Geordie Ridley's song was Parker's Horse Drawn Omnibus and the events predicted in the song actually took place, it is believed, in 1861 and not in 1862, for the song had already been sung before the second Blaydon Races. From the Cloth Market the bus moved along Collingwood Street, which was not too different from what it is today. It then turned into Scotswood Road past Armstrong's factory and onto the Robin Adair, not the now rapidly deteriorating closed building near Scotswood Bridge, but much closer to Newcastle town. And, as the song tells us, at the railway bridge the bus wheel flew off. Speedy repairs were made and the bus continued its journey to Blaydon Races, while the injured went the other way to the Dispensary, to Dr Gibbs' and to the Infirmary.

Dr Gibbs was one of Newcastle's best known doctors, who had his surgery at the bottom of Westgate Road. Gibbs' Chambers is still there today next to the Savings Bank, but the infirmary, sited at the car park close to the new Redheugh Bridge at the Newcastle end of Scotswood Road, has long since disappeared. The Dispensary, a small building in City Road close to the Pilgrim Street roundabout is also no longer there.

Still, as the song says, twenty-four people did carry on to the Blaydon Races. Paradise was a delightful place in those days. The River Tyne was clean, so clean that salmon were frequently caught in the reaches of the Tyne close to Blaydon. Armstrong's factory at Elswick (the Scotswood factory had not yet been built, nor had many of the rows of houses stretching up the hill from Scotswood to house the factory workers) was one of the few buildings around. The banks were covered in grass, woods and flowers. Streams flowed down into the River Tyne and animals roamed undisturbed while children played nearby. Horse-drawn traffic trundled along the cobbled road that went to Blaydon Races.

Today only the name remains although the area has been considerably cleaned up in recent years. On the river side, the railway line which took the racegoers to Blaydon Station has been pulled up and the narrow stretch to the river is being developed as an attractive industrial park.

So Parker's Horse Drawn Omnibus continued along Scotswood Road, across the Suspension Bridge, replaced now by a modern one, and right into Blaydon Town. The Chain Bridge, built in 1831, was pulled down in 1967 and the Mechanics' Hall at Blaydon at the end of the 1970s, whilst, of course, Jackie Brown is long since dead. Oh, yes, he was a real person, quite a character in fact. He was, as the song says, the bellman of Blaydon. He was also the town crier and the verger at the Parish Church of St Cuthbert. But none of these jobs brought him any money. This he received from doing a little advertising for various individuals and firms. Geordie Ridley employed him frequently to persuade people to go and see his show at the

Mechanics' Hall.

So the twenty-four passengers alighted from the coach and made their way across the barges to Blaydon Island. Here they saw four races in all but the afternoon was a disaster. The first race had been due to start at half past two but shortly after midday torrential rain began and by the start of racing the place was a quagmire. Only one horse, Royal Oak, had managed to cross to the island, the rest being stranded on the bank by the rising of the river.

Incidentally, Geordie Ridley had written his song before this time so could not have possbily known about this storm and yet one verse mentions it, so it must have been added later than 1862 when the song was first sung at Balmbras Music Hall. Coffee Johnnie had a right to ask 'we stole the cuddy?' because the horses did not arrive until after four o'clock. Coffee was an amateur boxer, John Oliver, by name and when he died in Blyth in 1900 his body was brought to Winlaton churchyard to be buried with all his racing compatriots. By the time the four races were run most of the people had left the island and travelled home. Two years later the Blaydon Races stopped for the second time and the island in the river was deserted once more.

Colonel John Cowen had been in charge of the races on Blaydon Island and he always looked forward to starting them for a third time. As he owned Stella Hall on the south bank of the river not far from the island this seemed as good a spot as any to try yet again in 1887. You can distinctly see where they were run, although Stella Hall is no longer there. Most of the site is the Stella Power Station, but some of it is still green grass.

On this site the Blaydon Races continued until 2nd September, 1916. On that day crowds congregated to watch another day's sport, celebrating the success of their hard work at the Scotswood Road factory of Armstrong Whitworth. What the crowd saw was the first race, which turned out to be the last one. Anxious Moments, the favourite, won by a comfortable six lengths but was disqualified for carrying wrong weights. People looking forward to their winnings were to get nothing. The munition workers, the miners, the soldiers on leave rioted and fought amongst themselves. Booths were shattered, buildings were destroyed and it soon became pretty obvious that no further races would take place that day. The horses were led quietly away from Stella Haughs to await another year. At that particular moment no one knew that the Blaydon Races had come to an end. As a local comedian said in a song he wrote and sang to the tune of the Blaydon Races –

Oh, me lads, nee more yee'll see us gannin
To pass the folks on Scotswood Road
There's never nee one stannin.
There's nee more lads and lasses there,
Ne one te taak their places.
There's not much left of Scotswood Road
And nee more Blaydon Races.

So said Frankie Burns, and so say all of us.